A Dark Wood

T0318122

Written by Caroline Green
Illustrated by Gaby Verdooren

Collins

a wet, dark wood

a red coat with hood

a wet, dark wood

a red coat with hood

rats turn and dart

bats loop in the dark

rats turn and dart

bats loop in the dark

moths curl and zoom

dogs bark for the moon

11

moths curl and zoom

dogs bark for the moon

🐾 Review: After reading 🐾

Use your assessment from hearing the children read to choose any GPCs, words or tricky words that need additional practice.

Read 1: Decoding
- Turn to page 2. Draw the children's attention to the word **wood**. Remind them of the two different sounds that /oo/ can make.
- Can they find any other words with the short /**oo**/ sound? (**hood**)
- Repeat on pages 7, 10 and 11 for the long /oo/ sound (**loop**, **zoom**, **moon**)
- Turn to pages 6 and 7 and ask the children if they can find two words that sound nearly the same (**rats and bats**). Ask the children if they can hear the same /ar/ sound in the words **dark** and **dart**.
- Look at pages 14–15 together. How many things containing the long /oo/ or short /**oo**/ sound can they find in the picture? (*moon, loop, zoom, mushroom; hood, wood*)

Read 2: Vocabulary
- Go back over the three spreads and discuss the pictures. Encourage children to talk about details that stand out for them. Use a dialogic talk model to expand on their ideas and recast them in full sentences, as naturally as possible.
- Work together to expand vocabulary by naming objects in the pictures that children do not know.
- Challenge the children to describe, in their own words, how the animals move. Point to the following phrases and ask: How do they move?

  Page 6 **rats dart** (e.g. *rats run along*)

  Page 7 **bats loop** (e.g. *bats circle/go round and round*)

  Page 10 **moths zoom** (e.g. *moths fly fast*)

Read 3: Comprehension
- Turn to pages 14–15, and ask the children to describe what they can see. Prompt them to describe details from the book. Ask if they can recall what the animals are doing. (e.g. *the rats are darting, the dogs are barking*, etc).